Dino Disaster

Written by Merle Pyke
Illustrated by Stacey Johnson

Dino Disaster

Dedications

Author: To all the little dinosaurs out there, may your imagination soar as loud as a T-Rex`s ROAR! I dedicate this book to my grandson Landen, my son Kristian, and my good friend Miss Tang. And to my wife, who inspires my stories and fills my life with joy.

Illustrator: I want to dedicate this book to my children for always motivating me to do my very best. Thanks for always having faith in me.

Dino Disaster

Introduction:

Landon, a boy with a heart full of adventure and a head full of dinosaurs, is about to embark on a journey that will take him beyond the pages of his favorite books. He's got a brand-new T-shirt with a fierce Tyrannosaurus Rex, but little does he know, this isn't just any ordinary dinosaur.

This dino is about to come to life, and the school is about to be transformed into a playground of roars, stomps, and belly-aching laughter. Get ready to meet a dinosaur who's more playful than ferocious and discover a friendship that's bigger than life itself!

Dino Disaster

Landon woke up with a jolt, his eyes wide with excitement. Today was the day! He scrambled out of bed, barely able to contain his enthusiasm. He raced to his closet, his heart pounding with anticipation. There, hanging on a hanger, was his brand-new T-shirt – a glorious, vibrant red shirt with a fierce Tyrannosaurus Rex printed on the front.

Dino Disaster

The dinosaur looked ready to roar. Its teeth were sharp and white, its eyes glittered like emeralds, and its body, rendered in a magnificent shade of green, seemed to burst off the fabric. Landon couldn't help but gasp in awe.

This wasn't just any T-shirt; it was a masterpiece, a canvas of his wildest dreams. He carefully pulled it on, feeling the soft cotton against his skin, and he couldn't help but grin.

Dino Disaster

He stood in front of the mirror, admiring his reflection. The dinosaur seemed to come alive on his chest. He reached out and touched its powerful jaw, imagining the dinosaur's mighty roar shaking the ground beneath his feet.

Landon couldn't wait to show off his new shirt. He hurried downstairs, two steps at a time, his T-shirt flapping behind him like a tiny flag. He burst into the kitchen, his face beaming with pride. His dad was already at the table, sipping his morning coffee.

"Dad!" Landon shouted, "Look at my new shirt!"

His dad looked up, his eyes widening in surprise.

"Oh, Landon," he said, "that's a fantastic shirt! You'll be the coolest kid in school!"

Dino Disaster

Landon grinned. He was already feeling cool just wearing it. He knew this shirt was special, and he couldn't wait to share it with the world. He grabbed his backpack and dashed out the door, his steps light and his heart filled with joy. He was on his way to school, ready to conquer the day, all thanks to his new T-shirt and the roaring Tyrannosaurus Rex that graced its front.

Dino Disaster

Landon's heart thumped like a drum solo as he stepped onto the school grounds. His new T-shirt, with its ferocious Tyrannosaurus Rex, felt like a suit of armor. The dinosaur's teeth were so sharp, its eyes so fierce, it made Landon feel brave and ready to conquer the world. He adjusted the bright red shirt, feeling the fabric against his skin.

Suddenly, a shiver ran down his spine, making his teeth chatter. Landon looked down. The dinosaur on his shirt was moving! Its eyes blinked, like tiny headlights switching on and off. Its jaws snapped shut, making a click that echoed in Landon's ears. Then, the dinosaur did something truly unbelievable – it leaped off his shirt!

Dino Disaster

Landon watched in astonishment as the dinosaur, now bigger than a small car, landed with a mighty thump on the pavement. It let out a roar that shook the windows of the school. Dust swirled in the air, and Landon could only stare at the magnificent creature that had just burst from his T-shirt.

Dino Disaster

The dinosaur, sensing Landon's amazement, let out a playful roar that was more like a chuckle. Its tail swished back and forth, like a giant whisk, sending a breeze that ruffled Landon's hair. It was a remarkable sight – a real, live, and incredibly mischievous dinosaur in the middle of the schoolyard!

Dino Disaster

The dinosaur stomped towards the school entrance, its massive feet leaving craters in the ground. Landon, feeling a mixture of fear and excitement, followed close behind. The dinosaur was like a whirlwind, sweeping everything in its path.

The dinosaur paused, its eyes gleaming with mischief, and pointed its massive head towards the school's main hallway. Landon knew what was coming. This was going to be an adventure of epic proportions.

Dino Disaster

The hallway, usually filled with the chatter and laughter of students rushing to their classes, was now a scene of utter chaos. The dinosaur, with its massive size and playful energy, had become a whirlwind of mischief. His thunderous roars echoed through the corridors, sending a wave of surprised gasps and nervous giggles rippling through the crowd. His tail, like a giant whip, swung back and forth as he ambled down the hallway, accidentally knocking over a water fountain with a playful swat of his leg.

The fountain, once a refreshing source of water, now stood in a puddle of its own, its spout pointing accusingly towards the ceiling. The dinosaur, seemingly unaware of the havoc he had caused, continued his journey, his eyes sparkling with mischief. He lumbered past a bookshelf, sending a stack of books tumbling to the floor in a

Dino Disaster

cascade of colourful paper and stories. A chorus of "Oopsies" and "Look out!" rang out as students and teachers scrambled out of the way.

The dinosaur, completely unfazed, stopped for a moment, his head angled in curiosity, and sniffed at the air. His nostrils flared, and he let out a playful snort, his enormous body trembling with laughter. His laughter, a

Dino Disaster

sound like rumbling thunder, reverberated through the hallway, adding to the already chaotic symphony of shrieks and giggles.

The hallway, once a familiar and comforting space, had transformed into a playground for a playful dinosaur. It was a scene straight out of a children's book, where the impossible was happening, where laughter and surprise were the only responses to this unexpected spectacle. It was a moment of pure joy and bewilderment, as if the world itself had taken a sudden, joyful turn, allowing a dinosaur to wander through the halls of a school, leaving behind a trail of uproarious laughter and surprised faces.

Dino Disaster

The gymnasium doors swung open with a bang, and there he was - the T-Rex, his colossal frame filling the doorway. The room buzzed with excitement; the rhythmic bouncing of basketballs suddenly silenced. A hush fell over the gym as all eyes turned to the dinosaur, who stood there, blinking his giant, amber eyes. He looked around the room, his tail swaying with curiosity.

Dino Disaster

A giggle escaped from a little girl in the corner, and then another, until the gym was filled with nervous laughter. The dinosaur seemed to grin. He reached down with his enormous claws and scooped up a basketball, its size dwarfed in his hand. He lifted the ball high above his head and then, with a mighty flick of his tail, launched it towards the ceiling! The ball bounced off the rafters and came down with a soft thud, rolling towards the center court. The gym erupted in cheers and applause.

Dino Disaster

The T-Rex roared with delight, the sound booming through the room. He bounced the basketball again, sending it soaring high into the air, then twirled around, his tail whipping around the gym like a giant, happy dog. The children couldn't contain themselves, their laughter filling the air, and they began to clap and cheer. The T-Rex, loving the attention, started to do a little dance, stomping his feet, and swaying his hips. The children joined in with some mimicking his movements, while others danced around him, their faces beaming with pure joy.

Dino Disaster

The air was alive with excitement, the gymnasium transformed into a playground of pure dinosaur delight. It was as if the school itself had become a part of this extraordinary, chaotic adventure.

Dino Disaster

Suddenly, the dinosaur, began to shrink just about the size of a desk, lumbered into Miss Debroah Tang's classroom. He was like a playful puppy, bumping into things and causing mischief. His tail, like a giant whip, swung back and forth, knocking over a colourful display of student artwork. The children gasped, giggled, with their eyes wide with wonder. However, Miss Tang, she was not impressed!

Dino Disaster

The dinosaur, however, was oblivious to the chaos he was causing. He reached out with his giant, scaly paw and nudged a towering bookshelf. The bookshelf, overloaded with books about dinosaurs, toppled forward with a loud crash, sending a waterfall of colourful pages raining down on the classroom.

A chorus of excited squeals erupted from the children. Books fluttered through the air, landing on desks, chairs, and even the heads of the surprised students. It was a book blizzard, a delightful flurry of knowledge and adventure.

"Oh, wow!" shouted Gracelynn, grabbing a book about a T-Rex. She was enthralled, her eyes sparkling with excitement. Another boy, sporting a mischievous grin, caught a book about prehistoric insects, its pages buzzing

with illustrations of colourful beetles
and terrifying scorpions.

   The dinosaur, watching the
children's joyful reaction, let out a
deep, rumbling chuckle. He seemed to
enjoy the mayhem, the children's
delight making him even more
mischievous. He nudged another
bookshelf, causing it to lean
precariously, as if it were about to
tumble over and unleash another book
avalanche.

Dino Disaster

The children cheered, their voices echoing through the classroom, filled with the joyous noise of a room transformed into a fantastical playground. For a moment, the classroom was a chaotic yet wonderful whirlwind of laughter, books, and a dinosaur with a playful heart.

The dinosaur lowered its head, its enormous eye scrutinizing the eager faces before it. With a soft snort, it released a gentle puff of air, reminiscent of a light summer breeze, causing the children to giggle as their hair danced in the wind. It felt as though the dinosaur was granting them a whimsical blessing, promising a day filled with pure, enchanting joy.

Miss Tang, who had been observing this moment with interest, spoke up.

Dino Disaster

Miss Tang, who had been observing the scene with keen interest, interjected. "It appears we have a new visitor today," she remarked with composure. "Could anyone share their favorite dinosaur book with our new companion?" Instantly, all the students raised their hands enthusiastically.

"Landen, does your new friend have a name?" Just as the dinosaur settled onto the floor, its tail coiling

Dino Disaster

around the chairs and desks, it listened intently as the children began to share their beloved stories.

"His name is Elmer," Landen announced, but just as he introduced his new companion, it suddenly disappeared. Landen felt a pang in his chest. He looked down at his t-shirt, where the dinosaur was once again illustrated, its teeth bared and a glimmer in its eye.

Dino Disaster

"Landen, where has your friend gone?" Miss Tang asked. "Right here, Miss Tang," he replied, pointing to his t-shirt. The class gasped in surprise before erupting into fits of laughter.

Landen

The End!

Dino Disaster

About the Author:

Merle Pyke is a children's book author who loves to create stories filled with imagination and fun. He finds inspiration in the everyday world, from the adventures of children to the wonders of nature.

Merle Pyke enjoys spending time with his loved ones, reading, and exploring the great outdoors. He hopes his stories bring joy and laughter to young readers everywhere.

Dino Disaster